AWAKE

Poetry for the Healing
Felicia Clark

Measure Life In Bookmarks LLC

AWAKE

FELICIA
CLARK

Published by Measure Life In Bookmarks LLC in the United States.

This book is (mostly) memoir, reflecting the author's present recollections of experiences over time. Names, characteristics, events, dialogue and timelines have been changed for artistic storytelling purposes and to protect the privacy of those involved.

The author received permission from Paramount to include Star Trek elements in the poem *Mattress*. This permission is limited to the poem's inclusion in this book, and all rights remain with Paramount.

All writings and designs within this book belong to the author.
Cover art by Kayla Lulloff
Content edits by Kristen Mears
Interior pages by Felicia Clark and Kayla Lulloff

AWAKE: Poetry for the Healing
First Printing, 2025
Full-Color Paperback: 979-8-9919827-0-2
Black & White Paperback: 979-8-9919827-3-3
Full-Color eBook: 979-8-9919827-2-6
Black & White eBook: 979-8-9919827-1-9
Library of Congress Control Number: 2025900351

To all the women who woke up
especially

Kyla Morris
My best friend, fellow survivor, and healing partner,
who always reminds me to awaken my power within.
Thank you for letting me be "the one who stayed."

Kaitlyn Kenealy
My therapist, healer and SHEro,
who was the first of us to wake and learn
how to use her magic wand to hug the brain.

CONTENT WARNING

Remember: Your mental health is a priority.

If you need it:
Take a break.
Seek support.

You matter.

Triggers:

Abuse
Addiction
Anxiety
Death
Depression
Grief
Loss
Mental Health
Rape
Reproductive Health
Suicide
Suicidal Ideation
Surgery

Table of Contents

AUTHOR'S NOTE

Dear Reader,

If you found my book and feel compelled to read it, then I can assume you are someone who is haunted by the past, looking for an escape, or seeking connection with an author who bleeds onto the page. Whatever reason(s) drew you here, thank you for immersing yourself into my passion project.

This book has been decades in the making, so I'd like to share a little background about how it was conceived.

In 2018, I started therapy at 31 years old. By the time I called to get added to a waiting list for mental health support, I was so deep in depression, anxiety, and unhealthy patterns that I feared it would be too late to escape. I completely stopped writing, fell into the clutches of substance abuse, isolated myself from community, and lost my sense of purpose in the world.

Two years later, when the pandemic shut the world down, I doubled down on my crutches to numb any thoughts and emotions too heavy for my heart. While it was one of the darkest, loneliest moments in my life, it was also an enlightening time that launched me on a path toward self-discovery. When I moved from porous boundaries to rigid ones, I found peace in removing myself from toxic relationships and situations that, before my healing began, I had tolerated in silence or ghosted for safety. As I slowly crawled toward healthier choices, I noticed that the people leaving my life no longer understood me, but the people showing up were on a similar journey. These were people returning to my life or finding me for the first time. Some, of course, were meant as further lessons, but others have since become part of what I like to call my Support Squad.

In 2021, I signed up for a Wide Open Writing retreat in Maine, where I spent a week with empowering women writers. I shared that my creativity felt controlled by some recurring themes, lessons, people, and settings. The group defined those pieces as my *Obsessive Writes,* telling me to never stop writing them until it brings me closure.

When I returned home, I started combining my Obsessive Writes into one document. The pieces were in fragments, quotes, short stories, novellas, and unfinished novels. Eventually, I decided to rework them into the form of poetry. Each painful memory was written alongside my healing moments, giving me an omnipresent view of what I'd been processing with my therapist. While I believe the poems stand on their own, I'd also been seeing vivid imagery as I wrote them, which pushed me to include graphics. I branded each section with its own visual component, from the innocence of childhood in watercolor, to the darkness of trauma, to scrapbook collages of healing, to a combination of the three in renewal.

I chose to publish this as a collection of poetry for the sake of having some level of privacy for my darkest moments while still feeling I could exorcize these stories from my soul once and for all. Finally, I feel like I can *rest* this body of work *in peace*.

Please note that because a lot of what I experienced was at the hands of other unhealthy and abused people (myself included) who also deserve grace, I have changed some identifying details, settings and situations to protect their privacy as well.

So what is my hope for this book?

My hope is that by releasing these poems to the world, it will unleash the other stories that have been trapped beneath them.

What do I hope for you, fellow reader?

I hope these poems free you from any fear or shame you may have of your own story and allow you to heal from it.

Finally, this book is also for those of you who can't stop

purging darkness onto the page. Don't stop writing what possesses you, because it is the only way to freedom.

You are worthy and deserving of happiness, and I hope you find a glimpse of it by the end of this book.

All my light and love,
Felicia Clark

INNOCENCE

7:46 a.m.

I overhear them discussing
the day I came—such a blessing.
So frantic and fickle, the memory stirs:
my exit, a wintry blur.

The roads heaped with slush,
damp as Dad's coaster discarded in a rush.
Like a burning celebratory cigar
dropping warm ash in the car

I slid into the world,
my arrival causing trouble
for their poverty-line finances
but still they took their chances.

Held in Mom's arms, I reached for my carbon copy,
feeling separate now from my first body,
always in waiting, wondering
if I will make it to another Spring.

tombs

A plush neon brontosaurus
nestles in the soft grass,
bright among his unusual family:
Mom's gray, velvet ring boxes,
snatched from her nightstand.

I transform them in my hands
like a puppet master. Two at a time,
my arms become their long necks.
They speak through the opening
and closing of my fingers.

The reptilian guardian swivels
her giant head back and forth
like a graceful swan, searching the trees.

This mock mother presents
a perfect green Maple leaf,
sunbeams projecting shadow veins.
The little hatchling wears it proudly,
its center arcing like a rainbow,
curling at its wilting tips.

Those who wear the star of the trees
won't outlive this Jurassic summer.
I lay them out, open at the hinges,
burying them beneath sawdust mountains
in the stuffy garage graveyard.

In the cool evening I find dead branches,
carve cracked mud parcels,
freeing fossils from their tombs.

constellations

Dad packed the blankets in the truck bed,
and Mom heated hot cocoa on the stove
we drank from a Stanley thermos.

It always works out.

Below the Milky Way belt, we're hypnotized
by the glittering velvet sky, waiting
for the next diamond—so bright, we swore,
we could hear its streak
flashing shadows on the grass.

A damp quilt on our backs in summer
or frozen cheeks and toes in winter,
Dad never let us miss a show—
school nights be damned.

Sleep when you're dead.

He was the Captain of Constellations,
and I, his trusty Navigation Officer.
Together, we set our sails, following
the W of Cassiopeia or the tail of Draco.

After the Capricorn king retired,
only those on the A list were welcome
to adventure with the Aries princess—
a rite of passage to her heart.

One day closer.

eggshells

cold and crusty wake up
mom's in perfume and makeup
from eggshells and dresses
i count the fences
along the highway
as dad drives us away
like the drag racers
to the weddings and benefits
sister cries and i shun her
mom holds a cigarette out the window
i wonder what will come of this foreshadow
from the back seat
i know all of this will repeat
soon everything will calm again
but inside remains
our discomfort and confusion,
for there's no time for reason
seeking high fives and good vibes
from friends unaware of the diatribes
the rampage is past
but peace will not last.
we pretend anyway
because that's our way.

¡ay, caramba!

Among the cans of fructose-laden soda
and BPA plastic bottles of spring water,
I ride beneath the cart.
My reflection stares back
in the chrome grates
that print scarlet tattoos on my legs.

I shiver in the brick-floor section
where the frozen foods dwell.
I shed a layer on the linoleum floors,
cruising past cocoa-dipped granola bars,
lime-green dill pickle jars,
dried ramen noodles and boxed spaghetti
with powdered sauces
abundant in added sugars
and non-iodized salt.

Every time Mom stops
for packages of instant mashed potatoes,
cartoon-themed cereals,
giant cans of green beans
or canned meat substitutes,
I play a game of chicken.

When my fingers catch
under wobbly rubber wheels,
salty tears turn sweet
with a sticky ice cream sandwich treat
to hold me over until dinner.

I don't remember
when I had my last ride.
I don't remember
when I pinched my last finger.

topographic tales

From picture books with squeaky pages,
creaky hardcovers and vibrant illustrations
to young readers with crinkly paper,
fragile binds and flimsy covers,
to YA novels with short chapters,
cardstock jackets and textured titles.

Ink fades like sun-bleached tattoos
on saffron-stained pages.
Each was a signature brand.
Though we move on, distrusting
the verbal stories, these paper languages
stay stuck, memorialized on fallen trees
like an open-air tomb—

it is here I get lost on purpose.

contact

I kneel on pea-green carpet,
outstretching my torso.
My hand connects to the glass,
scanning the screen for Vega.
I taste dusty electricity
as white static zaps my fingertips.

Frozen, I search the room
for evidence of a change
in universes—
a crossover of dimensions.
Then stare in a television trance
dizzy from the wormhole.

The doctor returns to Earth.
Recorded radio frequencies prove
her trip through space-
time was real.

I still wait for a coded
message of my own.

life size

Authenticity was easy
when I belonged in the world,
a safe space for innocence
to play before incidents.

I biked rubber to puddle,
hands-free, arms to sky,
reaching for universal truth,
head back, trusting destiny.

I picked figurines over dolls.
Perhaps because I was my own
real-sized replica,
cranking music on her boombox,
recording favorite songs on tape,
performing plays for ghosts.

Author Doll wrote stories
on construction paper,
penciled illustrations
on raggedly stapled pages,
and read aloud to her plushies.

Then falsities claimed me—shattering
innocence like the glass ceiling
in Successful Doll's mansion.
The world was now a stranger,
too intolerable to belong.

I skid skin to gravel.
Magnetic tape snapped
in my cassette player.

Scissors unevenly chop
Receptionist Doll's hair.
Unfamiliar touches return;
I torch skin and pages.

Time broke its promise to heal,
weeping wounds left exposed
without scars to gel on the surface
to seal the survival tonic below.

I toss Charred Doll aside,
merging hands with little,
life-size Me.
She clings. I guide.
We embrace. We cry. We walk.

foreshadowing

Whatever animal the cat dragged in,
we gathered round it with sticks,
watching its small chest rise and fall
with the writhing of maggots.

We carved the carcass
like wild beasts—stabbing
and studying anatomy,
watching the world of slow decay
in Earth's oven light.

Our sticks were scalpels,
revealing lungs between ribs,
punctured sausage-rope intestines,
and mashed-potato brains in cracked skulls,
like a middle school science project.

Of course, it could never happen to *us*.

debt

ONE hops on the handlebars.
TWO pedals blindly down the street.
ONE tries to guide TWO.
TWO swerves, trying to peek around ONE.

ONE
Watch your right.

TWO
Huh?

ONE
Watch out!

Tires skid.
Brakes screech.
Metal clashes metal.
The bike scrapes a bumper.

ONE is plastered to the rear window
and slides down like a cartoon character.

ONE and TWO
wake from their shock
and can't stop laughing.

A screen door creaks open
and then slams.
THREE rushes out,
his shaggy, curly hair bouncing,
checking his car for damage.

ONE and TWO leap
off the warm concrete.
TWO bikes away.
ONE runs away.
THREE yells and chases.

2 YEARS LATER

ONE and TWO
walk the halls
of their new high school.

ONE pokes TWO.
TWO jabs ONE.
ONE and TWO
skip down the hallway,
laughing around a corner
and—collision!
with a head of hair.

THREE stares down at them.

ONE and TWO
flatten like pennies
under his gaze
and scurry away,
squeaking like mice,
to the girl's bathroom.

ONE
Oh my god...

TWO
Do you think he remembers?

They find a sticky note
on the bathroom door:
You owe me.

TWO
Yeah, he definitely remembers.

Giggles echo down the empty hall.

the pyromaniac

From ferocious flames to smoking cinders,
he tried to burn the town—a restart.
She wanted to save the village swindlers,
but their choices forced her to depart.

She swore she'd stop desiring to give protection
but his gaudy ankle bracelet captured her attention.
She agreed to see him only to push a new direction
when he intended to earn her affection.

She fantasized what tensions wrought his soul
after selecting another object to control.
Scorching and torching all commodities to charcoal,
his basement a collection of all that he stole.

His smudged hand gripped a ring,
carved from chopped logs that Spring,
the painstaking pile he'd ached to ignite
but loved instead, engraving in the night.

They cling to each other in the rain,
an umbrella from their solitary pain.
His offering opens her lips
so thin like a partial eclipse.

The town stood tall for another day
because she asked him to stay.
But soon he found himself misled,
for she had suddenly left him ghosted.

Her choice sparked fear alone in bed,
terrified he'd come for her head.
He imagined she'd kept the ring, forever unwed.
It was all that stopped him from a furious spread.

tree rings

The Maple tree began to rot
like their marriage. Each leaf
tainted the next, and the sun
charred heavy black holes
into the tree star centers,
knocking them from knotted limbs.

Every year, the disease reached further
until no leaves could regrow—
a balding trunk, limbs barren
even on summer days
like an empty nesting mother.

No more blooming spring buds
or fiery autumn cycles.
No more shade for the home
or protection from the storms.

Dad chopped it down in large chunks,
exposing the innards of the stump.
I watched from the rose-tinted windows
as his axe carved the rings apart.

a carving

It began in elementary school:
a compulsion no one,
not even I, could understand.
I used pencil erasers,
friction forming a pulpy "A"
against deep primary
blue
red
green
yellow notebook covers.
Then more of the same,
scrawling pencil to page,
meaning nothing then.

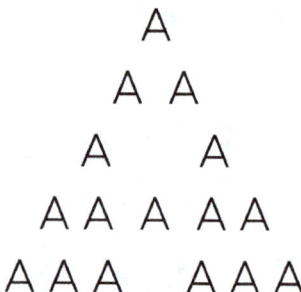

Years later, I brought
someone else's child home.
From the bottom stair
we locked eyes,
her disassociation weakening
with every step, survival
stifling her innocence.

Her mom never showed...
again. The grief is too heavy.
She drops
sobs
slaps
wails,
a song for the woman
meant to give her shelter
from life's storms,
now my responsibility.

She has a full belly,
a belly of laughs,
and a stomach for pranks.
I read to her while she traces
imaginary letters
over her moon and star
pajamas. In that moment,
I remember the notebooks
strewn across my bedroom floor,
covered in A's.

She sleeps to the sound of my voice.
I turn on the fan to trick the silence,
brushing textured curls from her eyes.
I wonder what fitful memory
will wake her tonight.

Crudely carved into her headboard,
I notice a letter. She shifts
in her sleep, covering it with her hand
like a safety blanket,
her fingers tracing its shape. A—
her first initial, imprinting
her existence on my heart.

moon eyes

She emerges with the stars,
slinking with silent paws
across the lawn, weaving
between shadowy craters—
the lunar landscape
mimicking her amber irises
split by crescent pupils.

The cyclops moon scans Earth
as she looks up, eyes mirroring
her twin reflection.
Nature is clever that way,
meticulously mimicking stardust,
translating cosmos into bodies.

My own personal astrologer—
she is the divine feminine,
spiritual connection to evolution,
domesticated and wild.
She always chooses me.

My own personal astronomer—
she is instinctual,
investigator of the universe,
reflecting constellation maps
back to the Creator.

Morning comes
and Luna returns.

the yes girl

Through grocery store aisles,
I stretch my arms high to tug
yours low, needing you to steer
me as I avoid strangers' eyes,
counting the linoleum tiles
and leaping over cart skid marks.

Teachers ask easy questions,
I press sweating palms into my lap.
Fidgeting, I stare at desk carvings
or out the window at hungry birds;
accidental eye contact shrinks me
to invisibility in my seat.

Too many good manner lessons
train me to a life of obedience.
My mind screams *no*, my mouth
says *yes*—over and over and over,
again and again and again. I lower
my head in shame, recalculating.

I easily pretend to disregard
emotionally stunted adults
who make racist jokes and mask
their pain through contagious crutches.
I stay vigilant—marinating in distrust
and untruths portrayed as love.

Where does one store it all?
Hidden. Deep. Building.

I am Yellowstone, the overdue caldera
making way for its scalding geyser,
its burning chambers of soot and poison.
I finally make eye contact
with the cracks of the crater.
I let myself reflect in its pools
and bathe in its edifice.

HURTING

The Weight

Boys always wanted to touch.
They said this made her the dirty one.
She believed them because their fingers
stained her skin.

Their marks warned other boys
that someone had been there first.
Shame layered her like full-body tattoos.
Did their greedy hands soil, too?

Why was her only purpose to be touched?
Why was their want so heavy?
Why is this guilt so infinite?

Broken Record

same soul,
different body.
same fear,
different words.

i am the sum of
d   a   M agE
on a record.

scratches
invisible   to the eyes   that watch
me,
ready to resist.

it repeats—repeats—repeats—repeats
like my cracked skull
from his cold   eyes—eyes—eyes
clawing to my thoughts.

screeches
clouding my judgment.

i burst through its disguise   to reach the inky secret.

if I told you, you'd go mad
at what lies at his core,
rotting like banned cider   from a prohibitionist's bar.

just know... just know...
those who beg for it
don't want it after all.

Chaser

Tattoo-covered scars match the tiger stripes
slashing down the middle of every coaster.
Shouting over loud bass and crackling pool balls,
the resin bar top collects our stories and ashes.
I take a puff off his stubby, grape cigarillo—
the tip's cool wetness pulls me from my haze:
I hate saliva.

A good song ends everyone's banter at once.
Heads thrown back, patrons scream-sing the chorus,
asking why we shouldn't give love another chance.
The bartenders shake us for shots,
warning us this is our last chance.
I stand on my stool and tap the dangling light fixture,
it swings and strobes above our heads—
a nod of approval to our hole-in-the-wall's playlist.

Crashing the curb, talon scratches blight his ivory car,
insisting on his sobriety when he fled the scene.
Just breaking it in like that new guitar—or me.
Always, he had more slippery lessons to teach.

An expert in torment from afar, he lights up my screen
with flickering messages like an alarm—flipping the bird.
Every text gets more malicious and desperate,
but they are finally ineffective and I fear the ending.
Someday, we all have to give up fun for safety, right? I ask.
No one answers but the cubes dancing in my glass.

Saturn

He points to a gathering of black wings,
beaks fishing worms from the ground,
as we return from another road trip
through our sleepy town.

On his father's porch, my muse's fingers blur
with skilled strumming, vibrations mimicking
heartbeats—the ache in my chest is so sore,
I already miss the passing memory.

One last deft flick of the wrist, his eczema
palms severed where Jesus was nailed
to the cross—calluses split to the bone.

Heading out for bandages, the breadwinner
approaches. White-knuckled, my driver tilts
the wheel, knowing this abuser's intentions—
now a stare-down between father and son.

I sink into the tan leather seats,
shielding my exposed summer body
from those polluted eyes that lose with a blink.
As we drive away, I fear next time his kin will win,
getting his eager hands on my skin.

Matrix Lovers

Abuse disguised as affection—an anchor
... blue pill, red pill ...
Resentment replaces romance—a rupture
... true pill, dead pill ...

A grave lover binds me
behind an impenetrable glass ceiling
manipulated by a digital rain—
his green eyes an infinite trap
to stay with him six feet below...

Imprisoned in the darkness,
my mind no longer my own.
Intimacy suffocates me
in this coffin, I noose blankets
for an eternal escape.

He threatens to end paradise
by trying to enter it with a knife—
the only tool for removing rusty nails
from this cell or cutting the wires.

When I finally answer the riddle, I open
my cage from its hinges—like a ring box
stored in my mother's dresser drawer—
climbing back into a bodysuit of autonomy,
and I see it all so clearly...

Break-Up Letters

I
  don't
    want
      to
        be
          needed.

I, the fisher. Hopeful.
You, the leech. Hungry.
They, the fish. Silent.

You want me so badly it destroys beds,
you leave Rorschach stains on the mattress
and in blotchy bruises across my skin,
like the rash that riddles yours
I always worry I could catch.

Tearful confessions of coercion,
you choke me with your love
until I turn on myself.
When did I become the bullet
and you the ricochet?

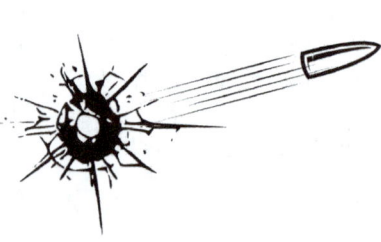

In paradise,
      I am washed away.

Crows Never Forget

The silence of unanswered calls
echoes through a labyrinth
of haunted halls. A murder
of crows caw and scream
as I walk, entrenched in a dream
toward this new prison.
I wonder then—has he risen?

Crows never forget: a curse
of the mind, doomed forever to regret.
They force their murky message
inside my head, a furrowed
ditch of wreckage. I can't
decide if their hollow eyes
are full of dangerous lies
or reflections of midnight skies.

All I can think to do
is frantically strike a few.
I fill my trembling palms
with jagged gravel stones,
their edges slicing new fate lines
the psychics can't read.

Rocks rain down like hail
on a suburban lawn, wings beating
furiously into the air like an elder
shaking out her newly sewn quilt.
The murder unravels
like an unspooling ball of thread.
A beak gouges my cheek
and I taste blood. They ask,

"What is it like being the reason
someone is dead?"

But then I see he is still alive—
his puddles sticky—a mess
of dried blood, like the vengeful
stabbing of the crow.

I serve hors d'oeuvres at a wake.
Funeral fingers smudge the vase
of a cremated stranger. He calls
and, apron untied, I answer.
His weathered body moves in whispers,
pacing his room in hospital slippers.
He says he does not belong
in this bed. The nurses are crazy.
He says I do not belong
in his family. He'd rather me dead.
I decide to make another call,
ignoring the cries of the crows
warning of his final fall.
I escape my own cage.

Years later, I stand frozen in darkness—
his scent hovers, inviting and dangerous.
I feel my hairs raise and molt.
I remind myself that he'd never
have set me free. That this smell
is just a memory. And so it shall
always be.

The Diary of HWSNBN

HWSNBN left me a dense, leather-bound journal
before he tried holding his own blood;
his skin torn like the pages he tried to remove
that clotted together with dried droplets.

The sheets intact were heavy
like an anchor meant to drown me.
Our initials repeated in jagged, irrational fonts
and obscure song lyrics with red notes
in the margins—it was hard to tell
what was blood and what was ink.

There's no going back to who I was before.
No such thing as unreading
what was written for the chords
in the faded pencil, a thousand
haunted songs with no ending.

We both quietly longed for paradise.
Mine was his words drawn into sand,
lovers' initials inside crooked hearts
that washed away with the next tide—
forgotten.

His was a permanent utopia,
somewhere he said I couldn't ever go.
Suddenly, I was a shell of myself,
an empty little bird's nest, a guitar case—
discarded.

She loves me.
She loves me not.

She loves me.
She loves me not.
It doesn't matter.
I love her.
It doesn't matter.

Brown House Prophecy

Multi-story and coffee-stained,
the house on the hill is covered
in a rainbow of wildflowers
and tall grass dancing on the breeze.
A splintering, wrap-around porch
overlooks a percolating creek.
It's dark inside but for a CRT TV.

His family stands in the living room.
There is an empty chair,
but I assume he is out with friends.
I accept water and sit stiffly
on an old, lumpy couch, wearing
my best smile at their jokes.
There should be more comfort here.

I wake up. Again.
From a time long ago
that never happened.
I scroll through my phone
and discover an announcement
that the one missing in my dream
is now gone in flesh.

I can't catch my breath.
I can't see the screen.
I should have known—

It was all right there, in that dream
now a premonition,
like a choppy film,
an unsolved riddle.

I long to go back
to that house,
that porch,
that family,
to shake shoulders awake,
make them see
my interpretation failure.
I long to ask questions about
the one who's missing,
the one nobody mentioned.
Now he is only remembered
in both worlds through memory.

Please Try

I follow you through the doors
you drew on blueprints,
a vision brought to life
by the hands of blue-collar builders.
How we wish we could do that
with your body.

Those murky blue pages
are like the ocean depths
our generation will never see,
the edges lifting with the breeze
like white-tipped waves.

I can see them so clearly,
as though I were a fly buzzing
around your head
that's filled with ripples
of brilliance
only a sticky summer night can bring,
both of us waiting
for a safe place to land.

Tonight, you lead me down
spiral stairs you envisioned
for yourself.
We loop down,
down,
down,
six feet down—
into darkness.

Who's to say you stayed there?

Perhaps you rose again—
no stone could keep you
locked behind a grassy gate.
Perhaps your spirit ascended
past the cold tombstone,
past the trinkets of memories,
past your weeping mother,
past your brooding father,
past your scattered siblings,
past your shocked friends,
past your childhood home,
and through my room.

To what do I owe this final visit?
I'm sorry I missed your goodbye,
too busy passed out on the floor
as you whispered, *please try*.

Of course, I was numb.
You know all about that.
It's magic.
Magic in the moment, anyway.
I wish you'd left some magic behind,
like Jesus leaving footprints
in the sand beside the sea.
See, seeing is believing,
and I didn't see.

Was it a familiar scene
when you found me on the floor?

Wait—
Where are we going?
Another of your buildings?
I see your precise sketches,
and fingers whitening around your red-ink pen.
You etched your heart in every creation,

like our Savior leaving a piece of fear
inside each of us, yet we crave more
until we come home—
tails tucked like an addict
giving in and asking forgiveness
one final time.

I imagine you, observing
another project complete,
sitting straight-backed in your squeaking chair.
Now, all I see is irony,
all those hours spent calculating stability
and strong foundations
while you drowned in rotting thoughts—
unsolicited demons for company.

What are you trying to tell me?
Where did you go?
Whatever, I've got more drinking to do.
You chose to stop, but I'm still deciding.
This one last sip might help me
make choices for tomorrow.

Don't judge me.
Let me *Rest*
and leave my body's imprint
in the carpet
In Peace.

Hey...
Tell me, are you safe?
Do you regret it?
I've always been curious
about my soul,
about my final destination.

When I dreamed about you before,

no one could find you.
I'd wake sweating,
reaching out my hand to—
what?
Grab you?
Catch you?
Pull you in from a parallel universe?

Is this all to tell me it's worth it?
Staying alive or dying?
Is there hope ahead, or eternal misery?
If the latter, well, *cheers fuckers*,
let's get shitfaced and live it up
before the end.
Life's a bitch, and then you die.
Isn't that what you used to say?

Why do I only dream of you when I'm sober?
What the fuck are you trying to tell me?
This time, you take me to the rooftop
through an unmarked door, revealing
a vast universe spread across rounded glass,
smudged, like we're specks inside a snow globe.
I never noticed these walls before.
But out there ... no limits, right?

The colorful gasses
and tumbling particles
bring a calm I can't explain.
If you stare long enough
you can almost see its expansion.
Suddenly,
I'm seeing.
I'm believing.
But in what?
What are you showing me?
I can't comprehend.

And suddenly, what even am I?
Some speck of dust.
Some lump of matter.
Some blob of energy.
Am I flecks of the sawdust my dad used to make
in his garage every Spring,
sawing wood to build your houses,
your skyscrapers,
your sturdy walls,
your protective rooves,
your doors,
your ... coffin?

I used to play with the wood shavings,
piled high like the rolling hills
of the Wisconsin Dairyland,
the pulpy grains catching
in the hairs of my sun-kissed arms.

It stuck to me like my traumas
because it was the opposite of trauma.
It was pure joy and innocence,
doomed to settle as nostalgia.

So, tell me.
What are we?
Dust, matter, energy ... sawdust?
None or all of the above?
More than the above?
Empty.
Whole.
Everything.
Nothing.
Complete.

No more pain.

No more yearning.
No more scars.
You worked hard
bringing your castings to life.

With talent like that,
why did you want to leave
so soon,
so young?
Did you know a secret?
Did you see the truth in your high haze?
Did you see the universe through snow globe eyes?
Can death really be so bad
when it takes you home?

When I arrive, will I recognize
the shape of your soul?
Does it have your body
from before the poison?
Does it have your face—
the same handsome features
all the girls giggled over?

Try to answer,
though I know I won't understand
until I follow you.
Can I follow you?
Would you take me in?

What's that?
No language can describe it?
Oh, do try anyway!
Please try.

in·san·i·ty

Burning cigars in bars
hidden like a scar—
a little gory
but quite the story.

Scratches on the car
unveiled like a new guitar—
a little breaking in
but quite the lesson.

Tormenting from afar
Glow up texts like a star—
a little aggressive
but not quite effective.

So Long, Heath(cliff)

Kryptonite finds himself tonight
in a hill-cave floating on the mist
above the Moors—this corpulent monster
lifts a moribund body to her righteous place.

Their touch is a wicked demise,
like freezing rain hailing onto skin,
evaporating from gray lips—
two bodies so pale, so weak,
yet their twin flame burns
with the strength of a forest fire
roaring through windswept trees.
They will flare out together
in one grave, buried between
jutting stones and griffins.

She gave him her youth.
He took her autonomy.
She'll expire in his arms.
He'll hunt her soul.
Neither shall ever be free.

The Diary of SWSNBN

It should have been me
who couldn't forgive
him. I can't forgive
myself. Reading my words cut him
as deeply as an angry quill
slicing at an atlas,
exposing every route that led us here.
His heart splayed before me
like an unfurled map—
roads as veins, the unforgiving creases
hardening to vengeful scars.
I wonder if I will ever get
to see him happy.

Unconscious

You were all pollution and no poetry,
your promises potent but empty.
You refilled my glass with poison,
seeking secrets I never had
to control the narrative,
to justify your actions and know
the words that would hurt the most.

Your grip too loose around my mind,
fingers slipping off my brain's jelly curves,
now tight around my neck, dominating
its most unconscious state. I thought
I was too old for this to happen.

When I woke, I peeled you out of me.
A part of me went with it. I lay as stiff
as your greedy weapon,
wondering if I could force
myself back to sleep.

Though my body was still, my mind whirled,
as full of emotion as your reaction
following the incident. Every word
etched onto my bones, glaring from the screen
like an exposed nerve in my gums.

You wrote about love as though it were holy,
when all you gave me were demons
and memories that fester like a chronic illness,
no matter how far the distance,
no matter how safe my next partner.

With no strength to warn others, I often wonder
how many women you wrecked after me.
How many had you conquered before?

The Oracle

I entered the home
of flower and fruit oils
so overpowering I teetered.
I slept to it;
I woke to it;
I was raped to it.

The smell of citrus
burned my lungs
the way oranges eat
layers of my stomach.

The morning after, she was there
in the shadows
this black albino oracle
like a Stephen King character
I read on the plane.

Her chrome pupils reflected
my wilting brown irises,
her face contorting
like a tongue touching a sour pill.
I could see the truth of my secret
in her misty, unblinking gaze.

"Are you alright, child?"
Inside I was
weeping
destroying
screaming
leaping…

Outside, I smiled with teeth.

She perched in her wheelchair
like a queen on the throne,
offering me freedom
for a confession.
But I turned my back
and left with him instead.

He drove me down city highways
busy with oblivious commuters.
If I only opened that door,
I could end it all.
I wouldn't have to pretend later.

Perhaps I arrived in this city
just to die in it.
But no,
I don't want to die in Texas.
It's the last place
I want my body to rot.

He called me crazy.
Who was I not to love him
in ways he expected of me?
While he worked,
I puked in every bathroom.
My body purged the gasoline
he'd pumped into me.

Outside the art museum,
inside the sacred garden,
he interrogated me.

He'd filled his holes with mine.
I burst into maniacal laughter,
the song of female rage.

It echoed off the walls,
through the garden gates,
upward to paradise.
A familiar sound locked in my vault,
a fresh sound to my ears.
And I realize, I've been here before.

As I boarded my plane,
I could see the divine figure
behind my blinking eyelids,
waiting for me with voodoo
and herbal witchery.
This time, I don't turn my back;
she points the way
and I obey,
and obey,
and obey ...

Empath

FOR LUNA MOON

i watch over mommy when she returns,
silent, dragging her suitcase up the stairs.
it seems heavier than when she left.
i mew for her attention, and it breaks her trance;
she smiles and picks me up for a snuggle,
but we're interrupted when mommy grabs the bottle
from the fridge, pouring piss-colored liquid
into her favorite, delicate glass. finally
she wipes her tears and climbs into bed,
where i wait with a flick of my tail.
i feel her heartbeat race as she sleeps,
sweating, twitching, groaning, her body skewed
diagonally on disheveled blankets.
she opens her eyes to check on me
and i gaze up at her from my nook between her arms,
my yellow orbs like two full moons,
hers like deep forests, tangled by roots—trapped.
she sleeps again, and i know
by her jerky movements that she's trying to run
from something i can't see, the same something
she tries to forget with the potion.
whatever it is, or was, it happened outside,
where i couldn't help her. sometimes i wonder
what would happen to her if i disappeared.
i call out to her when she's gone, so she knows to come back.
no matter how sad she gets, she never forgets to return.
no matter how sick my belly, i take her pain.
it's my job to recycle it into love.
i love her.
i tell her with every mew.

55

Apartment B

The ghost in that room
was future me,
warning me away.

I stare it down as I drive past
as though, if I forget,
it could haunt me again.
If only I could forget.

It used to lie dormant inside,
fermenting in my porous marrow,
congealing around my organs,
creeping into every passage,
ready to silence me.

This haunting sneaks up and in
when I least expect it
like an assault.

Insanity lets me watch,
lets it stay another night—
just long enough
to heat my cheeks.

The Ring

The boy who used to burn the town
grew up to see the man with the crown
at church. The hymns made him calmer
and had brought peace to his dying father.
His life now focused on healing sickness
and seeking God for forgiveness.

His umbrella-girl sat in the back pews
with carvings so grand they'd made the news.
She traced the cherub designs in the wood,
wondering if he'd held back as much as he could.
Who'd started the fire in 1999 as part of a joke,
leaving the small town parish nearly broke?

She was there when her ring bearer appeared
at the local bar with his bride, her cheeks smeared
with mascara. He dragged his wife inside,
dirty nails puncturing her hand,
to confront his past—the single girl still in demand.

"Did you ever find that ring I gave you?"
he asked, as though it still held value
greater than the vows he'd made at the altar,
where just last year he'd eulogized his father.
She lied with a shake of her head,
and didn't bid them well but left instead—

for she'd watched the ring burn in the firepit
where he'd worn elephant-trunk pants,
with fabric so wide it made her mom fall
in drunk laughter. He mocked her caretaker then,
so she cast him out now. That night, alone,

she saw her mother's reflection in her own.

Winter's End

That's the problem with death—
even the devil will be grieved.

One adult's oblivious oasis, deceived
by soft voices and smooth faces,
can be one child's hellscape—
rusting hearts leaving breadcrumbs.

They say the brain forces
amnesia onto childbirth, or else
women would never grant siblings.

When winter ends,
frozen secrets are doomed to thaw,
traumas surfacing like ancient diseases
from melting ice caps.

The child is now fully grown—remembering,
frightened and curled in a dark corner.
How to grieve that rotting rock
now hardening in soil?

The Final .

She seeks my attention like a neglected child,
swelling and aching, dripping and gripping
my resilient insides.

Her crumbs ooze from a hungry mouth,
like clotting leeches or algae in a lake.
I try to erase her mess but she's always hiding
behind the last word, like the finality at the end
of a sentence.

I used to hate her. Tonight is different.
Tonight, we snuggle on the couch
under a heated blanket. I squeeze
my arms to wring her out one last time
from my damaged walls.

As election results trickle in, we wonder:
Will we be allowed the help we need,
before it becomes illegal, too?

Chrome Cheers

FOR LYDIA

You left in a time of endings.
Mourners collected in pools on the grass,
dazed like autumn honeybees
fighting hibernation, exhausted
by summer's grief.

Pilsner beer offerings
brought me back to a
cherry wood casket, precisely
the length of you. The lid
was closed, so our imaginations
opened it, painting impact-bruises
on your olive skin. Your thin fingernails
coated in their final shade:
turquoise-chrome.

Out of respect to your elders,
despite my distaste for brews,
I cracked open my can,
its tink echoing
beneath the town weepers.

Every April, we reluctantly cheers
another missed birthday,
taking murmuring circle-sips,
we pour you a swig—
liquid bubbling into dormant grass
beneath the willow tree.

We decorate your grave

with the empty cans, then fill them
with red roses from your daughters.
Around us, branches perform
a spring wind song, blowing our grief wide.

These days mend us,
for just a split second—
almost as long as it took
for your life to end.

The Dark Knight of the Soul

Self-deprecating comedians peacock across the stage
in painted hats and camouflage masks, strangling
each joke with their microphone cords. She laughs
on command but no laugh lines crinkle her eyes.

Home, she dons the black cape and contemplates
her next great leap—a better rooftop this time.
When the garden flowers can't stop her,
she'll know she's ready.

Atop the rusty ladder, rainbow tulips sway
with petals spread wide, revealing barren pistils.
She stops and caresses their empty hearts,
then her barren belly, and chooses bed.

HEALING

Flameger

Set ablaze at birth,
I burned in a silenced rage,
threatening to spread.
My flame roiled

but I routed it
toward the waves,
to quell the quiver,
molder to ash,
and calm the crash.

I shall rise again
as steam, united
in the atmosphere
and, one day, the cosmos.

33

Like my first breathing day,
you came in discomfort, stinging
frozen faces, filling cracked boots,
soaking wool socks—
I was born.

You centered in the unfamiliar,
trading in lifelong bullies for healing friends,
gathering digitally to learn more lessons
on the outskirts of a pandemic—
I was growing.

You ended in change, tethering the beast
before Old Habit Anger can release,
reigning in what was once unleashed—
I was revived.

Mona Lisa Wannabe

"Smile more."
To smile or not to smile,
that is the question.

let them
question everything
make up
for lost times
fuck
the patriarchy
only consent
to smile
because you choose
no regrets

Uterus' Birthday

existing in the space between
a celebration of life
and the celebration of life that once was

soon she will be freed from Her swampy cage
only to expire in the cruel spaces between
pulsing plumping and silent sinking

from healthy, fleshy cells
to thickened dark blotches,
covering Her like liver spots

She has aged more maturely
than most others of Her status
even if She didn't always perform
the way society—or i—expected

i am still so proud
She did the best She could
it is all any of us can ask of those
we have housed inside ourselves

tomorrow i give birth to Myself.

Rewrites

Once upon a time, I ached
for one last epic kiss from your novel lips,
your calloused hands with the car-grease cuticles
wiping tears from my damsel eyes.

I wasted a decade with my soul trapped
on dusty, abandoned bookshelves,
my edges tawny like a telephone directory,
tearing as I waited for your return.

Instead of your warm hands wrapped
around me, I was tossed in a library dumpster
of unrequited love and set ablaze in a ritual
burning, my pages turning to a fluttery ash.

If only I'd really known you then,
known how you'd go down in history
as just another stubborn American voter
who'd remove the rights to my body,
forcing me to wear the red hood of blood,
marking a continuation of racism and war.

Oh, how I would have rewritten the story.

Life Lines

Hidden in a closet heaped with clean clothes,
there lives an even bigger mess,
one which didn't exist until 9 p.m.
on her birthday where she discovers
an empty bottle of vodka—the carcass
swaddled like a child in a pair of pants,
tucked behind a hoodie from their alma mater.

She turns around to see if he'd snuck
in behind her. But she is alone,
the house deafening without
his Golden Oldies records blasting.
She places the poisonless plastic
on the table, like a vase for flowers.

Doubt settles in, sitting across
from the counterfeit rent money
now filtering through his liver
that he owed her three months ago;
she makes the only reasonable decision.

Is that your final answer?

Poison

Sweet, sharp, burning sips,
like liquid candy mixed
with acid. My throat
explodes with heat,
the boiling pit dropping
to my stomach—
a reminder of my passions
wrapped in sedation.

When I try to swim to them
the poison kicks in,
my motivation flows out.
My soul sits there
so I sit in it, staring back
at all my yesterdays,
whimpering at the
...   loss ...
of ... .   time   ...

Self-Care

Nourish yourself despite their confusion.
Express your truth despite their discomfort.
Build healthy boundaries despite their knocks.
Accept your authenticity despite their judgment.
Control your reaction despite their emotional responses.

Grieve your losses despite the history.

Surgery

May the surgeon be
neurotic and concise
and the instruments
free of unpredictable
artificial intelligence.

May he see me
through human eyes
on the steel table
and never bionically
from soulless machine.

Control

From cloud
to ground,
your blanket pearled—
hiding all the world
behind a mask.
Now comes the real task:
to let go.

Temporary

Behind my eyelids, drugged in fentanyl
and anesthesia, I float through space,
moving slowly past stars, galaxies, nebulas, black holes;
so vibrant and new, I wonder if I'm heading to the light.

So I heave my eyes open and am overwhelmed
by the feeling of being alive, like a newborn
on birth day. I close my eyelids again to see
what my imagination will bring next ... black silhouettes
of people I've met, who no longer exist.
They appear against the light-polluted sky,
and I do not know what they want
or why they are so quick to leave.

My nurse wheels me down to recovery
in a new bed of paper, on sheets as thin
as my emptied insides. There, my person waits
for me in a disposable blue mask,
which shows only his concerned,
smiling eyes. I am loved I am relieved
I am happy I am joyful I am ready
to take on the world.

The pain kicks in after the pill cocktail moves out.
I stagger into survival mode, knowing this pain,
this dizziness, this discomfort
is temporary.

Morning Affirmations

Ladies.

You are not a vessel
for unhealthy men
to heal through.

Repeat.

And Another Thing...

You are not an ally
if you vote for policies
that harm their communities.

You are not Christian
if you judge
how others exist.

You are not anti-racist
if you oppose
Black history in education.

You are not a feminist
if you mock women
having equal opportunities.

You are not democratic
if you push your own agenda
that threatens others' existence.

You are not absolved of sin
with crocodile tears
and a PR apology.

Postpartum Part 1: Mom

As I wobble to the bathroom
one organ lighter,
Mom offers me her arm. I think
about how our bodies are emptied
of the same parts. Though my first
home was torn down, I am
grateful the foundation still exists.
Mom helps me shower and change
like I am a child again. When I caught
flu, or had panic attacks, it was only
her who could make me feel safe. She,
always holding my hair and rubbing
my back, would remind me,
It's okay; you're alright.

Postpartum Part 2: Me

I am number 999553,
like an unwoman in Gilead
who doesn't deserve a name
because of my wicked existence
being born a woman, the sin
of daring to think free will
applied to me and my flesh.

Motherhood is more
than biological beginnings.
After all, God made Lilith
from the dust of the earth,
granting her the same
independence as Adam.

Upon awakening, my uterus
became the embodiment
of an answer I've always known.
Through the unappealing
apple trees, I see the sunlight
as she did.

The choice I made
was the right choice,
because
it was *my* choice.

Exorcism

Once you've survived your own demons,
horror movies are tolerable to watch.
There's no more covering ears and eyes,
wailing, sleeping months on the couch,
all lights on, and racing up the stairs.
There's nothing new to conquer,
nothing more difficult than our own minds
possessed, not by CGI spirits,
but addictions, depression and self-hate.

P h a n t o m   F e a r s

She seeks the permanence in removal
of society's most desired body parts
to evacuate the words of greedy politicians
and past lovers echoing off their walls.

Flashes of captivity c i r c u l a t e
behind her twitching eyes each night,
tossing her in sweaty sheets, coating
her skin in snake venom.

She recognizes the ancient demands,
hearing the gruff voice of
Adam coercing his staff
into properties with no exit.

Autonomy reigns outside
the wrought iron gates,
beyond the apple orchard,
past the vines of serpents.

She escapes just in time.

And it was so.

She *made* it.
She made it.

RENEW

The closet

i bin abandoned dolls and stuffies,
wrinkled cartoon shirts, torn colored paper,
dusty leather heels and tennies,
so i can climb in. slowed breathing builds
my courage; my feet squeak the hollow,
bifold door closed. darkness.

this space is a time capsule, holding hostage
my innocence from thirty years ago—
that little girl in her life before
violating tongues and touches.

combing the berber carpet,
my fingers catch in the loops
and scratch popcorn-textured walls,
serrating my nails like lizard teeth.
shame enters.

i clamp my lipstick mouth closed,
and return to reality.
tear-drenched crow's feet
overflow, rinsing my stained smile,
and i wipe the saltiness
away
away
away ...

Into the light

My concert can koozie hugs my sweating beer
as we sit around the campfire up north—
the great midwestern woodlands sprinkled
in small towns and minds.

The fire glow kidnaps a chalky white Luna Moth
in its hypnotic dance. On humidity, it floats
like a spirit searching for closure. As quickly
as it came into view, it incinerates itself.
We gasp.

I wonder about its last improvised thoughts
as it accepted its fate to the flames.
Are they the brave ones?
What do bugs know that we do not?

Ouroboros

ash to air
air to droplets
droplets to puddle
puddle to pavement
pavement to gravel
gravel to powder
powder to wind
wind to mountain
mountain to magma
magma to charcoal
charcoal to dirt
dirt to lips
lips to lungs
lungs to blood
blood to body
body to disease
disease to death
death to ash

I am (still.) woman

Yes, I wanted to tell society to fuck itself.
Yes, I wanted to cry in my mom's lap.
Yes, I was terrified of permanency.
Yes, I grieved my loss of options.
Yes, I was also relieved by it.
Yes, I have/had postpartum.
Yes, I still have my ovaries.
Yes, celebrate my choice.
Yes, respect my lifestyle.
Yes, I can still have sex.

No, don't feel sad for me.
No, I haven't been misled.
No, I am not in menopause.
No, I never wanted surgery.
No, I never wanted bio children.
No, I never wanted endometriosis.
No, I don't dislike working mothers.
No, I don't hate you for having kids.
No, I don't detest stay-at-home moms.

I celebrate every woman's choice.
This was mine.

Waves

The constant fight:
against each other,
like ravenous beasts striving
to be the first to take a bite of sand.
For each other,
like a village trying to escape cliff prisons
to see what lies beyond the coast.
Some see the horizon
when the moon lifts the tides.
Some seek revenge,
pressure whittling their enemies smooth.
This is not freedom.
This is a cycle that must be broken.

Don't stay for the kids

Words trigger seismic tremors,
life-altering wounds
searing rifts into chests
and burning the hearts
bargaining with denial,
doubting the decades.

The kids know.
Their dysfunctional relationships
are proof enough.
Damn nurture over nature
and spongy hearts.

New beginnings merge
at mid-life junctions,
lining the future silver.
Inspect your soul.
Search through touch.
Learn by experiment.

Welcome discomfort,
knowing fear of this new path
is temporary
and worth the ache.

Boundaries

porous...
I was a dog person as a child,
like obedient pets with wagging tongues
who act upon command,
begging burglars for belly rubs.

rigid...
I became a cat person as an adult,
like my feline friend jumping into laps
purring with control,
staying as long as she wants.

healthy...
I found balance in healing,
like a forest animal expanding expectations,
rehabilitating injuries, avoiding predators
and trusting my instincts.

Fibonacci

Oh, great infinite, numerical spiral,
how your
hurricanes dance life into space
pine cones seed existence
tree rings count the age of rain
waves percolate the shoreline
conch shells mimic the sea
sand grains travel on the breeze

your sequence builds like earthquakes
sending rippled energy through the world

Culinary science

sand-crumb constellations wash away in pearly tips
as sea lice leap on a bed of beached carrot-peel seaweed
stretched beside mushroom-slime kelp baking in LED sun—
sea foam blows like tumbleweeds across the frothy shoreline
which blubbery seals chase in their floppy gallops
while slippery fish slide down black holes
of hungry whale throats, teeth like tines,
but it's the prehistoric, noodle-legged
jellyfish who keep all in line.

Mirrors

FOR MY SUPPORT SQUAD

Healing friends will reflect,
not project. Ask them
but prepare for the truth.

When they tell you to leave him,
leave him.
When they tell you to call your therapist,
call her.
When they say you're overindulging,
flush it, smash it, trash it.

There's nothing you can do
to thank your mirrors enough.
You will never forget
how they owed you nothing
but stayed, reflecting light
into your dark cavern
with group hugs
and sober adventures.

To your therapist,
who was always working on you
even when you didn't know it;
thank them for their tools
by using them daily.
Even if you buy another bottle,
or forget your lessons,
or ignore more red flags—
remember how she'd say,
"Give yourself grace."

A fostering

FOR A

With the chaos in this world
and in this life,
it is she who silences fears
with her visits,
which are never quiet
but always peaceful.

This teen is an age
plausible to strangers
that I could be her mother,
if adoption had been an option.

The infrequent moments we share
are filled with eager hellos
and tear-filled goodbyes.

I could never replace
these caregiving memories
for any other letter.

New wings

sprinkles of dust
particles in light

sticky pizza dough
squashes

flour
on my fingertips

Manifesting

Synchronicity is all around:

like running into an old love
at a random gas station
between your houses,

or a young girl in need
of the care you deserved
and she heals you instead,

or you swipe right on a safe
partner who helps you treat
your greatest wounds.

If you believe, it will find you—
a cosmos connection heightens,
a loose end tightens with the pulling
of the threads of fate.

Mattress

I met Spock on a warm May day
over local brews and burgers.
Noting the hairs on my neck stayed flat.
He was kind, calm and confident—
something I had never felt worthy of before.
We walked around the city, and I wanted more
of that Vulcan solace.

In Fall, I watched from the second-story window
as he carried my old mattress on his shoulders
and tossed it in the parking lot dumpster,
like he was carrying the USS Enterprise on his back.
His head was pushed to one side, veins bulging
and muscles flexing against the weight
of my traumas—marbled stains in the fabric,
as deep and heavy as a black hole.
It was him I wanted by my side
as I began laying my horrors to rest.
So I let him.
And I let him.
And I let him.

Now, we live long and prosper.

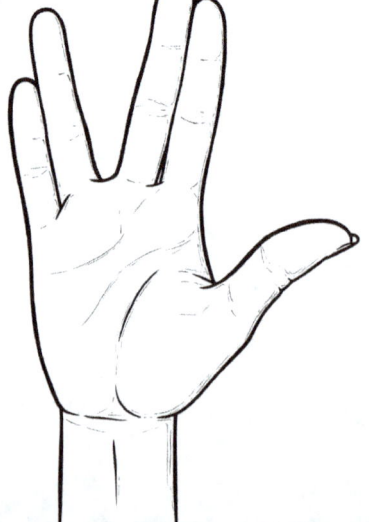

Breakthrough

What's vulnerability got to do with it?
Everything.
Literally fucking everything.

Nomads

From mossy forest to swirling sea,
dusty desert to soggy swamp,
steep mountain to tall-grass plains,
skyscraper city to corn-field farm;

From satellite internet to outer space,
empty water jug to filling station,
propane to dumping tanks,
overnight hosts to campgrounds,
gas guzzling to engine braking,
caravan cruises to solo trips.

From rubber to open road,
hiking to hydrating,
breaking down to repairing.

As we drive across the country,
we watch highway shoulders
give way to jagged cliffs.
Our hearts call out
for water, elevation and trees,
for sheltering cacti, restorative sun
and clean air—
all the elements needed for
freedom and healing,
which is the only full-time job
we were meant to do.

I want to kick my corporate keyboard
with these heavy hiking boots,
and crack all my screens on rocks
until capitalism's blood runs dry.

I want to live off this sacred land,
on a lake of clarity, and sit
beneath the safety of the sequoias
or sleep to the white noise of the ocean.
I want to see every immeasurable star
from the four corners of my house on wheels.

Sobriety

Soda rivers and boba-buoy oceans,
waffle-cone mountains and halved coconut valleys,
milkshake swamps and crumbled scone dunes,
asparagus pines and lemongrass prairies...

I am so hungry, I could eat the world
and savor every bite.

Aging

From construction paper
layered in pipe cleaners,
uncooked noodles
and cotton balls;

to cardstock trimmed
for business cards,
in neat stacks
or sweaty palms;

to printer paper
taken from the office
for a pile of resumes
fed on home ink—

our shell grows thin.

Soon, I'll be as flimsy
as onion-peel falling
from my fingers,
translucent as parchment
paper baking in the oven,
growing loose
in skin
and fucks to give.

Tomorrow

The only way out is through.
The only way through is today.
Today, I accept tomorrow.

Tomorrow is always a choice.

ACKNOWLEDGMENTS

Since the age of 9, when I filled every page of my first diary—complete with a lock and key—it has been my dream to become a published author. Now that this dream is a reality, I need to use as many words and pages as necessary to thank each and every person who made this book possible.

To my wonderful and patient partner, Vincent (Vinny) Seichter, for being my first draft reader, my NaNoWriMo cheerleader, and nomad adventurer. Without him, this book would not have been possible, thanks to his love and ability to play the put-together adult.

To my support squad Kyla Morris, Randi (Smalley) Strangstalien, Melissa (Kessler) Wells, Erica (Mazzolari) Bartsch, and Bryce Scherer-Brian for listening to my long-winded rambles about this book and encouraging me along the way. An extra special hug and thank you to Kyla for being my best friend, supporter, second therapist, first ARC reader, and biggest fan. I could not do half of what I've been able to accomplish without her perspective and blessing.

Thank you to my parents, Dave and Marsha (Roth) Clark, for encouraging my imagination to run wild when I was a child, letting me blast my music all night on my 5-disc stereo, and buying me an endless supply of notebooks and writing utensils to craft my stories and document my life.

Thank you also to my sister, Colette Clark, who often received the brunt of my childhood traumas but is now one of my best friends. I'm so grateful you are my sista!

Thanks to my therapist, Kaitlyn Kenealy, MA LPC, who joined me in my depths of hell so I could exorcize my demons and have a second chance at life. I will forever be grateful for your ability to heighten my frequency after every session and giving me the strength to "trust the process."

Special shout-out to my favorite writers and authors who

played a big role in my writing career. To Nikki Kallio and Laura Jean Baker for being my writing companions and champions. To Pam Gemin for educating me in women's poetry and showing me it was a form of literature worth pursuing. To Douglas Haynes who was empathetic during Hell Week in college and allowed me to bleed onto the pages in class.

To Rebecca Zornow, Leah Dobrinska, and K.L. Mielke for remembering my name and writing projects at author events, answering my late-night questions, checking in on my progress, and welcoming me to the Wisconsin author community.

To Dulcie Witman, Nancy Coleman, Linda Carleton, Sùsanna á'Kinlochaline, Susan Young, Bridget McGuire, and the rest of my Wide Open Writing crew for giving me the most incredible retreat of my writing career thus far, and for inspiring me to never give up on these stories.

To J. Allen for all the writer therapy chats. To Huckleberry Rahr and A.R. Grimes for answering my publishing questions. To Tracey Robertson who bravely shared her story and writing journey, which gave me courage. To Everalda Ocampo for giving me the confidence that my art goes beyond words.

Thank you to the countless educators who encouraged me to keep writing after their first read of my children's books, poetry, short stories, and novels.

I would not have had the confidence to publish this without the extensive edits and final approval from my brilliant content editor Kristen Mears, who also happens to walk the same steps as my British author idols. Thank you for making my poetry publishable. Cheers!

I can't imagine anyone better to design this epic book cover than my favorite artist Kayla Lulloff. Thank you for being my fellow bookworm, visionary, and sidekick. This book would have never printed without your help.

I would like to thank Julia Cameron for listening when the universe challenged her to create "The Artist's Way," which gave me (and countless others) the confidence and motivation to fulfill my inner creative's dreams. Thank you also to Taylor Swift for her *Reputation*, *Midnights*, and *The Tortured Poets Department* albums, which became the soundtrack to this book.

I was overjoyed when I received approval from Paramount to publish Mattress as it was written. This poem is so special to me and I am grateful for their legal team's openness to allow me to express my creativity in this way.

Lastly, to those who have gone from this world before me, I feel your presence and I take you with me on all my journeys. Especially to Lydia (Maiv nyiaj) Thao, my first poet and second sister in childhood (Kuv hlub koj!); to Luke Lindemeyer, my *awake* friend from the grave whose brilliant music helps me write; to Jenny (Harkness) Vanden Heuvel, who first published my words and would have likely been a book marketing partner; and to the "anonymous" soul that whispers to me in my sleep, "*Please try.*"

Thank you all from the deepest caverns of my heart and brightest pieces of my soul.

ABOUT THE AUTHOR

Felicia Clark is a literary fiction and creative memoir writer and published poet with her debut poetry book *AWAKE*. Her work has also appeared in newspapers, magazines, blogs, marketing materials, and multi-authored books. Through Measure Life In Bookmarks LLC, Felicia reads and reviews nearly 100 books each year and offers editing services to other writers. Her love of writing began at nine years old and led her to pursue a bachelor's degree in journalism and creative writing from the University of Wisconsin-Oshkosh.

As a nomad, she travels in a house on wheels with a home base in the heart of the Midwest, where she was born and raised. Follow more of her adventures at FeliciaClarkAuthor.com.